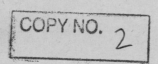

fraîchissant
 faire aime
égulièremer

Vit

IE '71

JUNTA

By the same author

BRINGING RAIN FROM CYPRUS

part 1

heat

white day

clarity

rears babies
& oranges alike

boiling lizards
scurry to dry rocks
for cool hideouts

that rising heat twitches
hills into shakiness

flowerless

white day

coup

winds assist the trees
in their songs

they are holding a fete
in the gardens
i hear spoons jangling
& glasses tinkling in toasts

our troops have surrounded
the palace
there is only one course
open to us
or so the generals tell us

the spoons fell to the ground
glasses were trampled underfoot
many died who were only guests

but many lived who had
never tasted wine

crockery

in the audience
sat a contingency
of engineers

who all night
guffawed & bellowed
like their own
bulldozers or diggers
engaging a
quarry gradient

their faces
were undefined
in the shadows

the performance
was almost scuttled due
to this seditious cabal

but their squawks
& brays were suddenly silenced

when a dancer
carrying a tray
of fine crockery
lost her footing
& broke every single cup

moor

the process hymns
   through its boymemories
wastes no young escapade
spares no mischief

    shadow slides
    hands to east men
& weather vanes

rolls fear in tight bundles
   around padded feet
          and i
remember bracken stews from
blue handled pans   cowards
 & hens

3 days of heavy sun
   a green radio pack
resting on tors
       until our snide
major handed us coffee & brandy
in enamel mugs   only to be told
     ' no tents tonight '

boat

scratched wild initials
on the rough hull
old & sandled
whiskered & lean
cold blooded fisherman
the boat jawed on

is warm loves jabbing
aegean sea in winter
marshalling low waves
treating white sand
while the sun heaves
a deadweight sunday

leered as the sails rose
sails marked fine
as the tawny ocelot
flicked a midge from his ear

see there boy
yonder in the bay
that is where you will
find your warm woman tonight
& your chilled wine

laughed a rope jerking laugh
to the molluscs

mast drooped long shadows
as we docked
5 old men in dialect
greeting him

be here at dawn
no gut aches and no fathers

lettuce

8 minutes every sunday
i check what looks like lettuce
in our garden

i'd certainly like lettuce to grow
there

very hubby tubby wife
midway between prototype designer
& production manager

she doesn't know
about the perhapslettuce or othervegetable
not yet
goodlettuce

with little shooting shooting leaves
soaks water from my saucer

very muchhyphenated son
springing rope tricks on me
& huge dives at me
he got bird bravery
oh lawdy dat wot he got

ah wilhelm march
baby march
month of lettuce hunting
& bubby finding

8 minutes every sunday
i check what looks like babies
in our garden

green bubbies   bush grown
            near the clothes pole

hyphen

the spaniard holds a welcome
for the granary halls
whosoever binds his hands
be he publicist architect
engraver or pilot
whosoever binds his goitred hands
attends the pogrom also

godchild of the sour malady
stricken the same

drawing up his accounts
tucking a desk elbow
under his breastbone
a subaltern
drawing up his accounts

4 for the colonel 3 for the major
1 for the rsm 6 for me

the subaltern
has a room
on his own
in a mess
near some others
but not too near
the mechanics the joiners the typists the warrant writers
the armourers the storemen the clerks the lance corporals who fill in form
all live in
all want out
all guard at some time
all sleep in the loo on their stag (near the jsiw)
all daydream
all scuff endless chippings on the parade ground
all suck
THEY SUCK
& the styx has wide arms for them

but my boy
my boy his voice
each time that inflexion

efficient and intense
(hears) it (smiles) it pulls eyelids shut
hyphenates us

fence

undermining the authority
of this garden fence
is a weather inflicted perplexity
which throws damp sulleness
and smoth grained sensuality
headlong at each other

the texture of this childhigh
wooden barrier alternates
between a dry warmth —
ably penal if transgressed
though less ably painted
and a rusty nail reinforced
constabulary of thin policeman
strips of wood
a sea smelling port for pirate bugs
or a shapely strut
for cobwebbing spiders

however
our vigilant lately much leaned on
garden fence encourages little interest
in our guests and even less
in the dog next door

debtor

when i leave my dreams unpaid
      or if i wake
in days when warmth is cosy
it is then   & only then
            that i can spin
with what our love is
      — or burn with what it's not

cans & pots shiver with
the calf heat
                  slightly goodbye
they murmur
                  slightly goodbye
as we evaporate in dear stillness
of your house
      where dreams are left unpaid
& sources rope beginnings

pferd

upstream draining
a black eyed vengeance
in 2 hoof scraped channels

his mane falls about
twitching ears
unwatched he steps
to lap water

they had stalked him
all that slow day
but with each cracking
of quisling twigs
or sudden wingbeat
of insect allies
he rallied with a
high flung head
and bolted

kestrel

a kestrel stalls upwind
the mice below select
their cracks & awnings

aroused by a wingbeat
to counter an air pocket
the kestrel sights
the last of three darting mice
on his downward swoop

the mouse hesitates
at an overhanging boulder
its head jerks to reverse
but he continues
to follow the leaders

the first grasp of the talons
brings blood spurts
from the mouth of the mouse

the other mice do not concede
they slink back to the wheat field

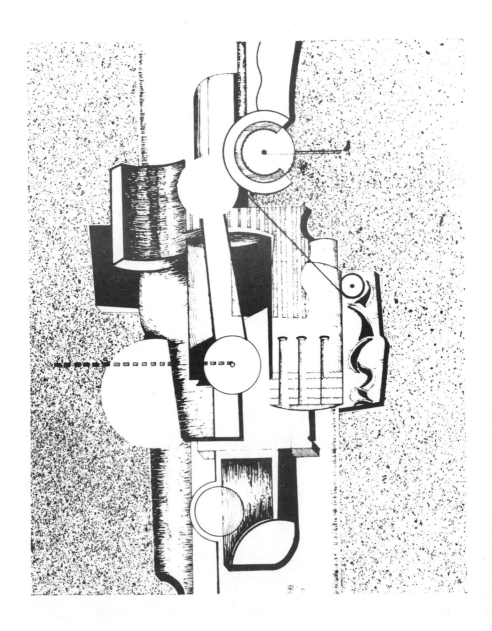

cards

reprieve came at ten o' clock
when the first of three riders
entered the camp

those who had marched
dipped swelling feet in the stream

those who had ridden
loosed tight neck muscles

for fear of attack
the commander trebled the guard

we extinguished what small fires
the cooks had made

in the night leaves rustled
and cold stars hastened away

with a yellow dawn
the horses were hitched to carts
whilst the footsoldiers struck tents

again that day
the land rose and fell
in steep hills and snug valleys

until the plain drew near
where Casal said our numbers would decrease

it was not until the evening
that we halted

four of the men played
cards round a large boulder

others wrote letters
or shaved

a sergeant yelled to the card players
about cleaning rifles

they argued over the small change
in the kitty

storicahr

sunday lay in
i tell my son
the story about
the 2 transvestite rats
that dressed as mice
so that they could eat cheese
then migrated to st paul's
for better prospects

he laughs at
their names
rodney rat & reggie rat
but i'm sure
all the time he's laughing
he's got slides of
bopping rabbits
projected on his mind-screen

étourdi

quand la cloche sonne
je me trainerai
comme un oiseau avec deux mains
autour des souliers doux
ou je gratterai le dessus des tables
avec mes ongles

si la cloche ne sonne pas
je resterai tranquille
comme un guerroyeur au tennis

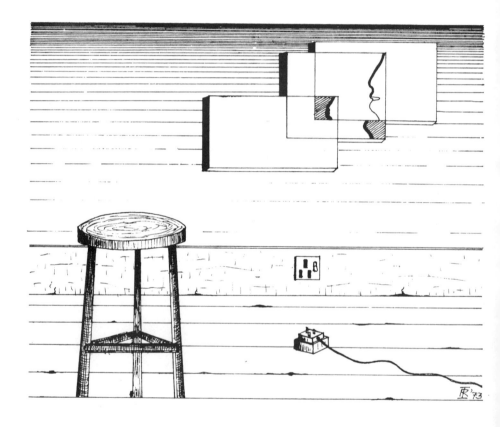

dancer

the glare of double light
attacks the positivists
crackling unsure

'believe me we'll starve for less
than gaston's parallel steps'

slop point of sparkle
scamp sun in a periwinkle winter
drilling into a hill
lugging grass up its sides

stringhorn scorned us
his plough scoring illegal notches
in a gracious field

the shares hack
the birds peck
dancers enquire where balance sleeps

so their music
with pipes and accordians
chants on the branches
folds on the stones
until staked to some petrified ridge
it fades

'your dancers slept in slight hollows
and i must have payment'
the dancers admitted

our bell player answered
from a painted cart
he paid the landowner his fee

at this the sky paled
rivers were misguided
dogs wailed and there
was green blood beneath barn eaves

winds had known no looser limbs
hedges waved above sheltering animals

in a circle of oak trees
the dancers whirled faster
the musicians played louder

and stopped

as a girl in bare feet
raised a torn blue waistcoat
high above the crowd

myriorama

high summer
the goatherds climb

they load sad donkeys
for the market
with thick skinned oranges
and sheepskins dark and odorous

white houses
have freed the days heat
evening plays
as the wadi settles

young girls clasp
gay embroidery
in the scented patio

the men sit in bars
their cigarettes stowed
on puddled tables
sandled feet resting
on straight wicker chairs

in the harbour
water beats
against dimly lit ships
greased machinery humming

the tourists
in light clothes
dance in night clubs
all the long night

a bitch in heat
howls on the beach and
a wild moon governs the island

phoenician walls
and roman ruins
frown on this
semblance of warless nightfall

the axis is split
a hundred years
are turning

significant

purpose takes septic brain cells
for walks along the harbour wall
clamour made by meddling waves
defeats
      tension claims a pilot boat
guiding a low tanker in the same
  stretch of inciting waters
hubbubing people and legend bells
brands of exciting matchsticks
        cornerly move
spear gut foe lighthouse
          dampen his fortunate
light bedouin sailors rebel
for yours is the kingdom of
    whale cuttlefish jellyfish
      and skate
all that in fishily motions exult
in or around farmed seaweed
    snakily flowing as
trinket lady hair   green haze
scale swimming sea when the moon is full and sorry
no sound betray for humans will seek parley
controllers of flame   fisheaters   breathers of air
inventors of net   gather your naval army
strong against
        junta and coup

icon

poets & their caprices
the composite man
waggling a whores tongue
at rats furnishing
the foundry incinerator
or smug gangways
chamfering the pier

but its much more
than just connexion
a refinement of our existence
a literary concubine

a squatters camp
in the early 50's
with flat batteries
in my fathers lorry
me in a pedal car
with fair hair

like someone
else you know

coal

sunday
midnight
monday

climbing the stairs
to bed

i go into my office
& imitate a poem
knowing i'd be snugger
in bed
with my wrapped up wife
& clear dreams

remember that
last unsure flame
from the coal

well it also
had a soft bed
to go to

but its vocation
was to burn

part 2

the cat that visits places

within the precincts of 3 nails
        are guitarists priests
            nurses & farmers
they eat bacon
with brown bread

        the priest he owns
a clay pipe with which he
relaxes after mass
        the nurse has a brother in law
who paints landscapes of bavaria
 in algiers
occasionally the farmer comes into town
        to buy rope or tools
        the guitarist closes his eyes
as his music intensifies

on the pavement there is
a creamy coloured cat wearing
a red collar   it visits
        the hospital on mondays
        the farm on thursdays
        the theatre on saturdays
        the chapel on sundays
and changes colour at each location

slight stress

the evening was clear
he pointed at the lamp shade
and made promises about the crosswind
wedged between a park pond sky
and silent damp grass we grew like tomatoes
in a sussex glass house
stressing against red skin

rain barrel

it's not for us to decide
where the guns should be fired boy

we are only shepherds
noise to us is the exciting aeroplane
that descends on its run-in
from the mainland — athens maybe
they tell me they even
have machines there
that suck away your dirt

turning to his cart
loading the fifth child high
on the knees of an older boy

no it is not for us
to tell you these things
we do not know of such things
nor the happenings which you hold
so important

yes — we see the soldiers
and we see them play football
after they chase our sheep
from their area

but no-one from our village
heard bullets
of which you ask many questions

Dimitrios who has an auto
said he saw turks with guns
but he is old he sees much
after a day in the bar

no boy —keep clear
my children grow impatient
we go now to the city
to visit traders who wish to buy
our skins and milk

perhaps the mountains
can answer your questions boy
many men ask mountains
when they are in doubt
many men do do.........

les yeux dans le théâtre

il y a bien des yeux
    dans le théâtre
mais ils ne voient pas
il y a beaucoup des globes
    dans la salle de classe
mais ils ne tournent pas

je suis ma plume lente
  vers le bord de la page
mais je ne tomberai pas
    seulement les feuilles tomberont
quand la saison triste arrivera
puis le monde tourne
avec son papier-monnaie ses rois gras
ses chats décharnés dans la ruelle
et avec les enfants maigres
    qui saisissent leurs meres
comme une arete de poisson
dans la gorge

la jonglerie dit et les prairies chuchotent
qu'il y a bien des yeux
    dans le théâtre
mais ils ne voient pas

le plus triste de tous les signals
de la mer ou du ciel ou de la terre

number 9

this house number 9 is where the dogs piss
on the worn carpet where the old man devours
an uninviting lunch from soiled plates
where the stomach turning stench drifts and hovers
like coastal fog around a sheltered bay
the wind has no authority here for windows
and doors are forever closed
the sun never comes to visit this house
and yet
a single rose has the audacity to grow
in what seems a poisoned garden

weighing against the bones of boats

once
my sloop boasted a full jib
that foreran a bulging mainsail

occasionally
the jib would be taut but excited by keen winds
its rhythmic billowing induced a drunkeness in the crew

unskilled
seaman that i was i left the polished helm
to fill my eyes with the jibs acrobatics

during
my punishment my teeth were tight
i was keelhauled five times

now
i live ashore and cast my rod from the harbour wall
and i lay hawk eyes on you little fish

soon
my hook will dive deep in your mouth
and my knife will slit the base of your belly

the laughter in the soil

men laugh on the balconies
and the laughter sheds
over tiles
seeping through the cracks
to hearten the soil

men continue to laugh
dropping like slaughtered livestock
when their laughter is depleted
no-one renews the men
no-one can laugh as vigorously

soon when all the men
are gone
pillars will replace them
pillars standing still and irrefutable
cold pillars made of marble

pillars are terrifying canes of bishops
pillars are fibrous shafts
connecting gods membranes
pillars are the outer tracts
of the religion of the phallus
pillars are hoists for pardoned souls

angels will cry
their tears funnel down
through these pillars into the soil
where the happy laughter will
be extinguished

it was the happy laughter
that concerned the government
and they condoned its extirpation
there was no place for heresy
in the country
the balance must not be tilted

but they overlooked the cycle
and the steam from the hissing laughter

rose slowly in fine mists
to drift above the pallid earth
and grapple with mountains
quite suddenly one day
it rained
it rained
it rained a heavy rain
a long rain
a very long rain
a rain of laughing men
falling without injury on streets
on housetops on market stalls

laughing men whose one desire
was to climb balconies

damp saturday

the sun
with a list of rain schedules
rattles its abacus earth

whilst systemizing
its joints bearings & mountings

cold in the park
grey statues
with faith in clasped hands
trail shattered feet
on shiny grit

the mud clogs
on my heels
& on the pram wheels

looking for a puddle
to wade in

the marks on our wall

from the landing
you can see marks at regular intervals
where our son has used the wall
to lean on as he climbs the stairs

the marks probably consist
of jam chocolate biscuits oranges
yogurt but chiefly of butter
however the marks carry
none of these products colours

rather they are murky grey
quite shiny & interestingly circular

3 bottles with elliptic pachyderm
(pour les sectateurs du surréalisme)

in the hothouse
spring plants
            surging viridescent blue
                        crocusmauve
                  tangerine/moonwhite

each gardener who enters
rinses a french flag
under breton's rusty tap

cools his neck
with the material
& proceeds to commit suicide

not one plant turns
from its agnostic pot
as gardener six shrieks deathsongs
they are too busy
avoiding an isochromatic state
                  pink to fishsilver
            blacklight
                        to
                        gold
                  maroon

yes pins were dislodged
makeshift pianos fell victim
to blockades & wars
                  to whalegrey
            d us k p   ur p le
                        black

et maintenant
dans le monde entier
nous marquons le pas

first ripples of a storm

wine & bread in small quantities
the dark descended
negative patches your pawnshop surrendered
in my ferocious triangle
i fastened to the furthest apex

soft the voices of trained slanderers
& holy men fell into the night
everywhere deep wells were filled
young men gathered around them
with coloured buckets & long ropes to draw

we pulled torn curtains helplessly on them
this nettled pact has rapist undercurrents
rewarded only by smooth skin tones
hell would ever curse & scrape
my imperishable ideals & needs

scrape & draw boiling blood from me
together with the legs of sheep
dangling the line would sway to catch
a flowering rifle barrel
hairgod ghost the burning powers festered

then rippling beneath me
my tide flowed & ebbed
building its waters higher
in preparation for the ultimate flood
that would drown your township
twice i matched the turbulence
of your violent lake with long oars
& sea skills that i have learned

yes twice i matched it
before the wine dammed my river

new house

it was a long withering day
as we walked with the man who
    calls names
  he had tears on his sleeves
  from the brambles and
frequently his hat was tipped
askew
    by the branches

the house he led us to
  had curved bricks
and a bowing chimney
    when he knocked on the
door with his stick

a beagle answered
    adjusting a green apron

a land i made love to

autumn purrs with long winds
and tight bicycle clips

from the train a trail of
flag washing busy under cliffs

twig brows wrinkle lawns
childs upturned wheels spinning

channel pressing thin breakwaters

merely conditional merely solid this
archetypal wind   devotional as
it chants the mass

take a stick and cap
for hikes through crisp leaves

ever slow this fellow winter
presents books of old jokes and tales
read in candlelit houses

lighthouse — a hitching post
for stars

begged fawn wallpaper dock
be gentle with her timid ship

watering place here sucks
herring and mackerel to slabs

fools fox only to hotel here
in this month   fools fox

step sleeping on that island
where moors do not begin
and seas do not end

chews time a thread unravelling
tugs hearts a land made love to

feeding the birds

they come
to fulfill
the contract of hospitality
with a pecking acceptance
of bread crumbs
tossed on the grass

& to combat
any sinking of dignity

hold heads aloft
like the clawing
of an upturned crab

a fruitless exasperation

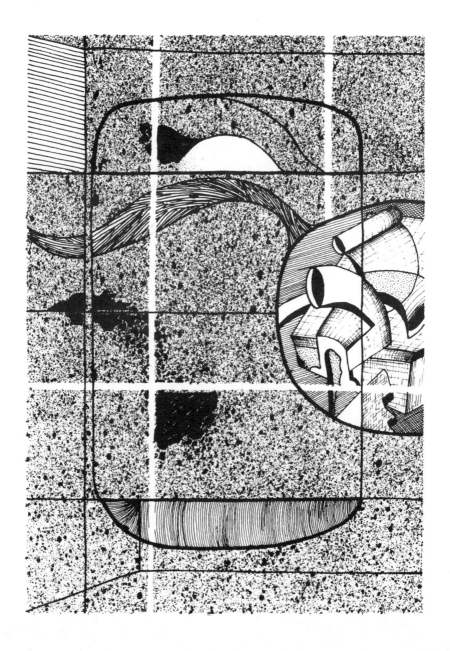

bring that cup in here

complaining of a virus
nightbones perished
          neil said it was unavoidable —
even for a nightbone
well eaglewild mornings might
   just as easily catch fever or
hazewind evenings might fall
with cracking eyeballs — who knows

neil was right   even at nursery school
he was right
          formidable at times though
musical   hated football   father came
from a l   o   n   gline of walls —
     india & the sepoys & all that
tarnished trash recollected only by
fathers of prospective lays   debs
     they call them i believe

odd that these fairycakes should
have currants & cherries astride them
i'd have thought only tiaras of golden
circles & rubies would have suited

rather than whistle

shoes pinch
on the road where loose
                    stones wake
to stiff brooms & shovels

            he may take
lights & stow omens
health charms & rings beneath
tree roots

there is never a hint
        of guarantee where flowers
are concerned
stokers would crumple dock flowers
seamstress girls would pluck factory flowers
students would bite university grounds roses
artists would dab purple on petals

ponies kiss wild moor flowers

sharp turns down shellons street
        meet the wind

must be protective
        this council plan
to construct rope ladders
up to the viaduct

passes the thought carriage
clicks to the margin

drives slowly
& it cracks barks zips & slashes
the high power wire
            tramcar dawns in glasgow

those special new years eve trips
        to noisy kelvin hall
our circus/carnival treat
excitement knew no better recipients

toys scattered the cars oh the cars
now it shames that there have been
    so few words for him
that would have been too simple
to live that love is so harder
        than to record it
& it boils my being into worm form

no speed

son
no speed
rest late
i call parchments
in your tale
robbers of sound
perfecting crime
for repitition

grandly hair & forecastle

you know
its time you came home

i've masturbated
& got drunk
to replace you

times i don't eat
nor take off
my coat
in the living room

slow introduction
to missing buttons
a guide line
to them ole statues
in the parish church

decides religion
is no longer
loose beads on a chain

the shelving of early page
books & the seizing
of husky precious minutes
the perimeter fence
not a toying with
sighs & eye rubs

talking to people
who shudder visibly
at the sound of drums

this heres the unmade bed
this heres open curtains
at night
this heres old scraps
of paper in a
cold fireplace

you know
its time you came home

outhouse

skins were drying
in the sun
a thickset peasant

picked an insect
in larval stage
from a gable

expressionless
he studied
its undersides
& returned it to
a grey boulder

his right arm
was bandaged
& a line of dry
blood cracked an inch
above his eye

the assasination
had been difficult
mistiming had brought
4 deaths
a house search
& harsher rationings
in the village

the peasant would
now hide in the dense
forests of the hill country

& there consult the arithmetic
of animals & woodlands

room

sunlight filters
through cracks in the door
making a plane of the dust

who am i
to rid the world
of cats milk
& cardboard box handles

strange confident he
handling solidbrain

soon evil   soon dog

accept pink eyes
for luck & safety albeit warmth

chat dans la gorge
where trains once shunted
or fish sang   fast
ratchet hand of lynx eye

all the thinking while
cruise cars/leaves/clouds
spotted room floor

holiday

mists clear
& valleys regain
bases for their trees

here in sussex
daylight jolts deep night
into lust dew morning
& near autumn sunlight
fumbles through branches

chessboard fields
feed sheep

poplars
tall wind guards
line the orchards
where women pickers
fill wooden boxes

we walked to the level
& crossed
its slow river
having no reason
for doing so

chirico's street

only chirico
saw streets as
clouds & worms
see them

he has turin by
its throat

a wing of horizontal aerials
crossed by great
hulks of cryptic shadows

arcades stifling their madness

sidewalks holding benches
that brood

nothing moves here
nothing is impending
nothing comes
nothing goes

white columns of
the porticos
the sand scuffing of
the unloaders
at the wagon doors

a girl
rolling a hoop
runs into view

it seems like terror

dien bien phu

I have no hope for you
turned out from a beating french empire
to elephant your way through
burning cities causing unspeakable grief
to oppressed refugees

I have no respect for
your para-military strategy
as you ensconce unwilling martyrs
in monsoon-threatened trenches
that breed gangrene in your wounded

neither do I have admiration for you
who ran with explosives strapped to your waist
to blow suicide gaps
in the french wire — yours
was a hellish passion nurtured by hatred

has anyone respect for a croix de guerre?
for the vulnerability of generals
too absorbed in military tactics
to notice rain clouds?
the chant de partisans goes on
I am still not immune to it all........

qui est jeu

uculent, audac... théâtral,
re des chefs chou... sé
t jamais de leurs arm...
aient d'autant plus redo...
nt peu ou pas le temps... lav
e à Versailles. Arafat, qu'... t dan
otte de la montagne ou da... n salo
re, est toujours botté, san... é par un
ang de cartouches à la P...cho Villa
de figure parce que pa... isé depuis
trois semaines. Le... ntraste est...
pp... ...ard qui sent qu...
...er et ses gé-Na
edes habillés sur ave
ccesseur. Puis, mas
e de la propa-tour
it de son second... n
e sur le pavois et dame
abes. A la même détac...
en Jordanie, à une d'obte
d'Amman, dans une l'évac
accroupis sur le sol, berté
e les doigts, écoutent cilités
s » du Caire. « Nasser, tion d
e, a été vaincu par l'aide flots
Amérique a apporté à Is-qu'en
ettant de se servir de ses matiq
Flotte ! » Les six hommes Nass
épaules. Deux d'entre eux loups

Aber Jewge...
Oberstleutr...
...chen Gehe...
erfolgreichs...
ebte zwölf Jahre lang unter uns
...r blieb unentdeckt, bis er zur
Nesten überlief. In seinem Ne...
Yorker Asyl erzählte Oberstleut...
...nant Runge dem STERN sei...
abenteuerliches Leben und da...

...nge 41-Jähr...
...stes KGB de
...sowjet...
...Moskaus...
...rarhe...